GEORGE BENJAMIN

MEDITATION
on Haydn's Name

(1982)

RELATIVITY RAG

(1984)

Studies for Solo Piano

Faber Music Limited

London

*Bärenreiter-Verlag, Kassel : Boosey & Hawkes (Canada) Ltd., Willowdale
G. Schirmer Inc., New York*

Meditation on Haydn's Name was one of six pieces by English composers
commissioned by the BBC to celebrate the 250th anniversary of Haydn's birth.
The first performance was given by John McCabe on Radio 3, on 31st March 1982.
The first concert performance was given by Paul Crossley at
the Cheltenham International Festival on 15th July 1982.

The first performance of *Relativity Rag* was given by the composer
at University College, Cardiff on 23rd November 1984. This was part of the
1984 Cardiff Festival, at which George Benjamin was the Composer-in-Residence.

Meditation on Haydn's Name and *Relativity Rag* may be
performed with *Fantasy on Iambic Rhythm* (F0948).

Duration: Meditation on Haydn's Name   2½ minutes
           Relativity Rag   4-4½ minutes

NOTES ON PERFORMANCE

The following pedal markings are used:

Sustaining pedal: ℘ed.   ✳

Third ("sostenuto" or "Steinway") pedal: III   III

. . . . . . ✳   indicates the gradual
                release of the sustaining pedal

✳   indicates a sudden, violent
sfz   release of the sustaining pedal

sfz pppp   indicates that the key should be
                struck forte and staccato, then
                silently re-pressed once the sound
                has naturally decreased to *pppp* (in
                this case, approximately after one quaver).

▷────o   indicates a diminuendo to silence.

⌐•⌐   indicates a short pause.

To Sarah Taylor

MEDITATION
on Haydn's Name

GEORGE BENJAMIN

December 1981 – January 1982

for Robin Holloway

RELATIVITY RAG

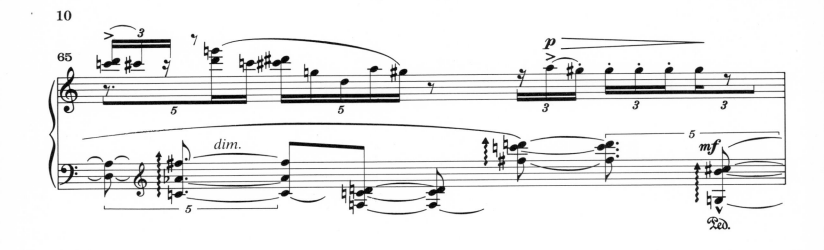

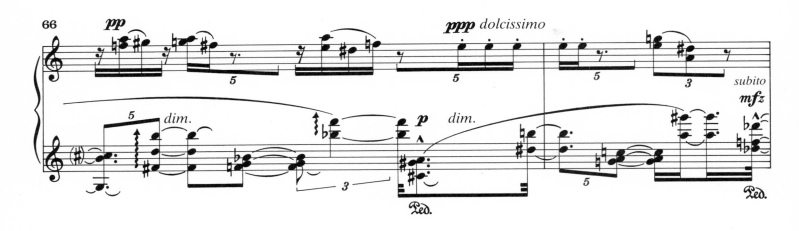

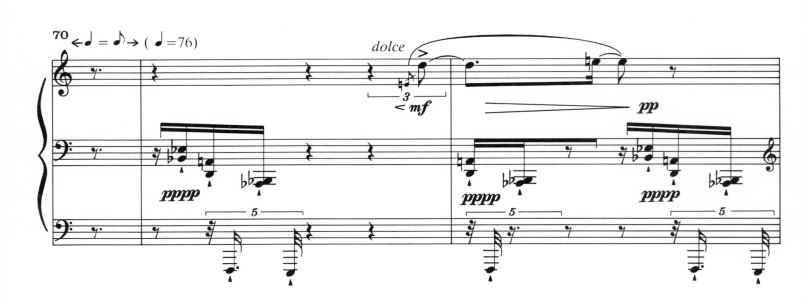

* The *sfz* followed by a dotted tie, indicates that the key should be struck sforzando and staccato, then silently re-pressed once the sound has naturally reached *pppp*.

* The sustaining pedal must be held down until the end of bar 103.

October – November 1984